ANTONIO VIVALDI

CONCERTO

for Flautino, Strings and Basso continuo
C major/C-Dur/Ut majeur
Op. 44/11
(RV 443)

Edited by / Herausgegeben von
Felix Schroeder

Ernst Eulenburg Ltd

London · Mainz · Madrid · New York · Paris · Tokyo · Toronto · Zürich

Ernst Eulenburg Ltd
48 Great Marlborough Street
London WIV 2BN

ANTONIO VIVALDI: Concerto C major
for Flautino (Recorder)

Pincherle[1]), Inventaire thématique No. 79
Rinaldi[2]), Op. 44, No. 11

The present edition is based on a copy of the score in the Biblioteca Nazionale Turin, Collection «Renzo Giordano», Musica strumentale Vol. III, 292r—301v, entitled «Con to per Flautino». There is no indication as to instruments in front of the first stave.

Pincherle[1]), Inventaire thématique No. 79
Rinaldi[2]), op. 44, No. 11

Die vorliegende Ausgabe stützt sich auf eine Partitur-Abschrift im Besitz der Biblioteca Nazionale Turin, Sammlung «Renzo Giordano», Musica strumentale Vol. III, Bl. 292r—301v; die Überschrift lautet: «Con to per Flautino». Die Instrumentenbezeichnung fehlt vor der ersten Akkolade.

The solo part may be entrusted to a recorder without any hesitation. All dynamic and other markings in brackets as well as dotted slurs and ties are additions on the part of the editor, the latter in general by reasons of analogy. The bass has been realised in its simplest form as a suggestion and for guidance.

Die Solostimme kann man unbedenklich einer Blockflöte übertragen. Alle in Klammern stehenden Zeichen sind Zusätze des Herausgebers, desgleichen die meist in Analogie hinzugefügten gestrichelten Binde- und Haltebögen. Die Aussetzung des Basses ist ein in die einfachste Form gebrachter Vorschlag.[3])

Im einzelnen seien folgende Abweichungen von der Vorlage angeführt:

1) Marc Pincherle «Antonio Vivaldi et la musique instrumentale» Paris 1948.

2) Mario Rinaldi «Catalogo numerico tematico delle composizioni di Antonio Vivaldi» Rom 1945,

3) vgl. dazu Walter Kolneder «Die Aufführungspraxis bei Vivaldi» Leipzig 1955, pg. 95 ff.

	Takt	System	Bemerkung
1. Satz			
	105	Viol. II	letzte Note c" statt d"
	107	Viol. II	letzte Note d" statt e"
2. Satz			
	11	Viol. II	2. Note fis" statt dis"
3. Satz			
	42	Bass	4. Note fis statt e
	45	Bass	4. Note a statt g
	68	Bass	6. Note g statt a.

Felix Schroeder

Concerto C-Dur

für Flautino (Flauto dolce), Streicher und Cembalo

I.

Antonio Vivaldi Op. 44, Nr. 11
(um 1675 - 1741)

EE 6321

4

55

59

63

6

8

12

II.

14

[Vcl.]

E.E. 6321

III.

16

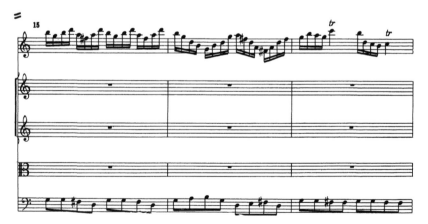

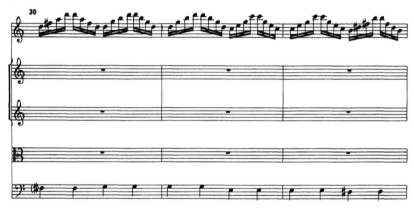